THE POCKET LIBRARY OF GREAT ART

Plate 1. SELF-PORTRAIT. *1886. Pencil. Collection Robert Lehman, N.Y.*

EDGAR·HILAIRE·GERMAIN

DEGAS

(1 8 3 4 – 1 9 1 7)

text by

DANIEL CATTON RICH

Director, The Art Institute of Chicago

published by HARRY N. ABRAMS, INC., *in association*
with POCKET BOOKS, INC., *New York*

On the cover
detail of A BALLET SEEN FROM AN OPERA BOX *(plate 27)*

Plate 2. BEFORE THE RACE. *1876–78. Pastel, Paul Rosenberg, N. Y.*

Degas

Though he is known as the painter of ballet subjects, Edgar-Hilaire-Germain Degas was far more than that. He was a portraitist of subtlety and distinction, a draftsman of infinite resource and one of the most exciting sculptors of his century. He was born in Paris in 1834 of wealthy upper-class parents, and it was supposed that he would follow his father's career as a banker. Edgar, however, had other ideas. On his schoolbooks he traced dream-heads and figures of knights in armor. He had a recurrent dream of his own: to be an artist.

Finally convincing his father that he was right, Degas enrolled in the studio of Louis Lamothe, a former pupil of the Neo-Classical painter, Ingres. At that time, Paris was drawn up in two hostile camps, the Romanticists under Delacroix, who insisted on emotional color and exotic subjects, and the Neo-Classicists under Ingres, who recommended a study of Greek and Roman art and practiced a hard, realistic approach to themes drawn from history and mythology. Degas was wise enough to correct Lamothe's dull teaching with frequent visits to the Louvre, where he copied the Italian masters; and he was soon to travel many times to Italy where he opened his eyes wide to the primitives and artists of the fifteenth century, like Botticelli and Leonardo.

Though he first tried to paint historical subjects in the approved manner, giving them what he called a touch of "modern feeling" by choosing more realistic models and arranging them in less formal poses, he soon gave up this idea and began to concentrate on portraits. Degas was a superb portrait painter; in his early canvases he immediately showed his skill in capturing the inner life of his sitters. A born psychologist, he enjoyed the play of one personality upon another. We see also his dependence on the clear structure and incisive drawing of earlier masters, combined with a feeling for discreet color and delicate effects of light. For all his portraits Degas made many drawings from life, then re-created his sitters from sketches and memory. As he progressed, his touch became lighter and he grew more able to catch the fleeting pose and

Plate 3. WOMAN ON HORSEBACK. *1860–65. Pencil*
The Louvre, Paris

Plate 4. THREE DANCERS. *1879. Charcoal and pastel. Collection M*

Webb, New York

transient expression. He never accepted a commission and never finished a portrait when he grew bored. When a beautiful woman wanted to pose for him he told her bluntly: "Yes, I'd like to do a portrait of you, but I'd make you put on a cap and apron like some little maidservant."

After the war of 1870, in which Degas served, he returned to find that the old society which he had loved was breaking apart. He looked around for new subjects and discovered them in the opera house and ballet. Here was the fluid movement, the flash of color and arresting play of light that he loved. At the same time, Degas became friendly with a group of young painters, among them Manet, Renoir, Bazille, Monet, and Pissarro. He took part in their discussions centering round painting modern life rather than literary subjects and stressing more and more daring effects of color. Degas disagreed, however, with these men who were to join with him in founding the group of Impressionists when they insisted on painting out of doors. There was more to art than surrendering oneself to nature, he said; one built a work of art *mentally;* through patient observation and style one carried it out. When he first visited the ballet, he recorded it in precise detail; soon he was changing and heightening his effects and substituting pastel for oil. Pastel allowed him to draw as he painted, and satisfied his desire for brilliant, more vaporous color.

At the same time, Degas sought new and surprising angles of composition. He tilted the floor of a rehearsal room; he peered down from opera boxes; he stood in the wings and glimpsed fresh, unforeseen slices of life. Part of this originality came from his

Plate 5. EDOUARD MANET WITH HAT. *1865–70. Pencil*
The Metropolitan Museum of Art, New York

study of Japanese art which was then the rage of Paris. From Japanese prints Degas learned to cut his figures abruptly, to overlap one by another—such devices being used to increase the apparent spontaneity of his vision, which actually was calculated down to the last millimeter. From photography, which he ardently practiced, Degas further discovered the close-up, the blurred background, and the sudden sharp detail, all of which he used for artistic purposes. And in his studies of dancers he re-created not only glamorous moments on the stage but also the hours of strain and ennui of the young girls exercising or waiting in the wings.

Degas applied his inventions not only to the ballet but to the race course as well. He had been the first to explore the action of race horses at the fashionable tracks near Paris where gentleman riders, brilliant in their silk coats, rode elegant, high-bred animals. He prowled round the city and came back from out-of-door cafés with trenchant records of singers and dancers. Again, it would be laundresses, working away at their monotonous tasks; or a series of women at the fashionable milliners. In all these Degas sought out the emphatic, telling line; his drawing became broader, more fluent while his color grew richer and more original as he left behind the conventional harmonies of the old masters. Until about 1886, Degas concentrated on one problem: how to combine the instantaneous vision of Impressionism with the undying principles of classical design. In many works his success was complete, but Degas was always a perfectionist, and in his last period he shut himself away from the world and tried to transform his style. He

Plate 6. STUDY: MADAME HERTEL. *1865. Pencil*
Fogg Museum of Art, Cambridge, Mass.

wanted to become a powerfully expressive painter, rather than the masterful draftsman. He took up sculpture in earnest and turned out several hundred strong, even rugged, statuettes of dancers, horses, and bathing women, all of them infused with a new violence of movement and rhythm. He studied the nude bodies of women in every conceivable attitude, twisting, turning, seen from above, from below, leaping from a tub, standing on one foot, sprawled on a divan. He re-did his ballet subjects, no longer drawing with pastel but plastering it on in one heavy coat over another. His final dancers have lost their piquancy; their faces are slashed with strokes of coruscating color; they look like strange, fierce birds or tropical butterflies. Much of this late style springs from the near-blindness of his old age. He could no longer see to work in the small; he needed to enlarge everything. On pieces of tracing paper over forty inches high, Degas drew vehemently. Gone forever were the delicate contours; the charcoal seems to dig deep into the paper and hew out form. Degas was not afraid to distort and to emphasize.

Personally, Degas was a super-sensitive, ingrown, bitter, and witty man. He had few friends, and to the end he remained a bachelor. An individual of exquisite taste, he had assembled a great art collection. In 1917 at the age of eighty-three he died, practically blind, and neglected by a new generation. He had instructed Forain that he wanted no funeral oration. "If there has to be one, you, Forain, get up and say, 'He greatly loved drawing. So do I.' And then go home." Thirty-five years later his place is assured as one of the most original artists of a great century.

Plate 7. STUDY: DANCE FOYER AT THE OPERA. *1872. Essence Collection John Nicholas Brown, Providence, R.I.*

Plate 8. YOUNG WOMAN IN STREET DRESS. *1872. Essence*
Fogg Museum, Cambridge, Mass. (Collection Paul J. Sachs)

COLOR PLATES

PLATE 9

Painted in 1867

HEAD OF A YOUNG WOMAN

The Louvre, Paris

Oil on canvas, 10⅝ x 8⅝″

With the simplest means Degas here made a living portrait of what a lesser painter would have turned into a mere study of a head. The face of this young, unknown woman is not conventionally beautiful. In writing of the women of New Orleans, the artist remarked: "The women here are almost all pretty and many have even amidst their charms that touch of ugliness without which, no salvation." Always seeking character rather than formal beauty, the painter has not minimized her largish nose nor corrected the slant of her left eye. The use of a few restrained tones (note how the black of her gown is repeated in the ribbon which binds her hair) and the subtle, delicate gradations of the rose and deep ivory of the flesh have created a remarkable work of art.

PLATE 10

Painted about 1869–72

DEGAS' FATHER LISTENING TO PAGANS

Museum of Fine Arts, Boston
(John T. Spaulding Collection)

Oil on canvas, 31½ x 24¾"

Auguste De Gas, the father of the artist, was a great enthusiast of Italian music and himself a successful amateur organist. Lorenzo Pagans, a Spanish singer, was celebrated in Paris, appearing in many concerts where he accompanied himself on the guitar. He often took part in musical evenings at the homes of Degas and Manet.

The artist has seized upon a typical moment, contrasting, as he often did, two different figures. The erect figure of the singer is opposed to the bent, aging old man, sunk in reverie; further contrasts are developed by daringly dividing the canvas by the vertical of the guitar and by silhouetting the profile of Pagans and placing the head of Auguste against an open sheet of music. The brushwork is made to appear casual and sketchy; there is relatively little color, tans, browns, grays, and whites creating a restrained harmony.

PLATE 11

Painted 1875-77

CAFE CONCERT: THE SONG OF THE DOG

Collection Horace Havemeyer, New York

Gouache and pastel on paper, 21⅝ x 17¾"

This is one of Degas' vigorous reactions to the night concerts he visited on the Champs Elysées. He loved to seize the exact gesture (here the singer moves her hands in a parody of a dog) and enjoyed capturing the disillusioned charm of such popular entertainments.

He has superbly rendered the right atmosphere, placing the profile of the singer strongly against a yellow pillar which daringly cuts the composition. The face, dramatically illumined by footlights, is contrasted with a repeated pattern of the electric globes.

Plate 12. SPARTAN BOYS AND GIRLS EXERCISING *(commentary fol*

PLATE 13

Painted in 1876

THE DANCING CLASS

Collection Harry Payne Bingham, New York

Oil on canvas, 32⅝ x 29⅞″

Degas began with cool and objective studies of the ballet dancers in the Paris Opera. In only a few years' time he advanced beyond the posed, static rendering of his first pictures into a world of movement and casual effect. This painting is broad and free in treatment, gathering many impressions into a remarkably complex design. All the bustle of different movements is caught with an almost camera-like fidelity. Degas cuts off one figure by another, overlapping his forms masterfully, but so shrewdly are they fitted together that there is no confusion.

Perspective is dramatically felt in the slanting floor and the diagonal line of dancers on the left, continuing back into the farthest corner, where some of the mothers are watching the class. Here Degas has added something new to art—a surprising view of a little-known world—composed with the grace and authority of an old master.

PLATE 14

Painted in 1876

ABSINTHE

The Louvre, Paris

Oil on canvas, 36¼ x 26¾"

This is Degas' most famous scene of café life. Shown in London in 1893, it created a scandal, the Victorian public being unprepared for so disenchanted a picture of Parisian existence. But these people are not really degenerates of the period; the artist had posed two of his friends, the woman a well-known actress and the man a distinguished etcher, in a spot much frequented by artists of the day.

The design is one of Degas' most brilliant inventions. From Japanese art he had learned this zigzag arrangement of lines which, beginning at the bottom of the canvas, is carried swiftly back by the flat table tops. The figures are placed to the right of the center and sharply cut by the frame. *Absinthe* is not, as the outraged Puritans of the day pretended, a study in alcoholism, but an Impressionist "slice of life," drawn with extraordinary sensitivity and painted with a deft, incisive touch.

Painted 1869–72

AT THE RACE COURSE

The Louvre, Paris

Essence on canvas, 18⅛ x 24"

Degas was among the first to paint the spectacle of the
race track. He loved the elegance of slender, nervous
horses, the gay silks of the gentlemen riders, and the
animated bustle of the crowd in the grandstands. With
an almost Oriental grace he has concentrated on the
silhouettes of the men and horses, subtly repeating
them in the shadows of the flat foreground. His vigor-
ously painted outlines give the composition a decorative
character; the repetition of browns in varying shades is
echoed in the grandstand and contrasted with the reds,
blues, and dull yellows of the costumes. Over all is the
pale, cool sunlight of Paris. Everywhere there is that
movement and unusual balance carefully worked out
from countless drawings. The final effect seems spontaneous, but the method was wholly calculated.

LIFT FOLD FOR ENTIRE PAINTING

DETAIL AT RIGHT

Painted 1876–77

CAFÉ-CONCERT: AT LES AMBASSADEURS

Museum of Lyons, France

Pastel on monotype on paper, 14½ x 10⅝"

In many of his scenes of café life one is struck by Degas' unexpected effects of lighting—the dazzling illumination of the stage, compared with the softer blur of the gas globes set against an evening sky and subtler reflections caught by figures in the crowd. This picture began with a monotype, a painting on a metal plate which Degas drew and then transferred to paper. Then he began to build up his color, balancing darks and lights, tones and hues, until his balance was achieved.

Here the design is extraordinary; we are thrust into a seemingly moving and confused audience and our eyes are led by the top of the bass viol and the brilliant red of the singer's dress to focus strongly on the stage. In such a picture, with its animation and shifting pattern of colors, Degas has suggested a whole side of Paris at night.

PLATE 17

Painted 1876–77

DANCERS AT THE BAR

Collection César M. de Hauke, New York

Essence on green paper, 18⅞ x 24¾"

A brilliantly conceived study for a famous painting in
The Metropolitan Museum in New York. As Degas
matured, his brush drawing became more flexible and
daring; he could now render his dancers with a sum-
mary power that no other artist of his period possessed.
Degas was often led to compare or contrast two figures
in action; here the dancer at the right is seen in the
violent stretching exercise at the bar; the one to the
left, treated more lightly and with less modeling, echoes
the pose with a more graceful practice position. Degas
often worked directly on colored papers of this sort
which give a strongly decorative effect when combined
with a few touches in flat oil paint. Like many of the
artist's preliminary sketches this one exists as a work of
art in its own right.

Plate 18. THE BELLELLI FAMILY *(commentary follows color*

PLATE 19

Painted in 1878

THE CAFÉ SINGER

Fogg Museum of Art, Cambridge, Mass.
(Maurice Wertheim Collection)

Gouache and pastel on canvas, 20¼ x 16"

Long before the invention of motion pictures Degas anticipated the close-up. Strolling along the Champs Elysées he dropped into the open-air night clubs where popular singers bawled out their vulgarities and was enchanted by what he saw. Unlike his ballet dancers, these entertainers are rendered with a sharp, satirical eye. He would do a whole series of them, eliminating more and more detail to summarize a moment and fix an unforgettable vision of footlights reflected on a rouged and powdered face.

He has represented this singer in a moment of intense action, with her mouth open in song, one black-gloved arm flung up for emphasis. The placing of the model in the frame is brilliantly studied so that the eye unconsciously completes the rest of the figure. The detail of the black glove was to haunt Toulouse-Lautrec, who adapted it to his many studies of the French singer, Yvette Guilbert.

PLATE 20

Painted in 1873

THE COTTON MARKET, NEW ORLEANS

Museum of Pau, France

Oil on canvas, 29⅛ x 36¼"

In 1872 Degas visited New Orleans to see his brothers who were in the cotton business and he lingered there to paint a few portraits and scenes of contemporary life. From moments in the Cotton Market he made sketches of about fifteen figures, weaving them into a picture which is not only a remarkable document of the times but also a series of shrewd and recognizable portraits. Each man is seized in some characteristic action: the elderly gentleman in the foreground who is testing a sample of cotton is Michel Musson, the father-in-law of René Degas, who is seen in the center, casually reading the local newspaper.

The unusual sense of space, the repetition of blacks and whites playing against the cool greens and tans, the brilliantly detailed drawing—all these elements combine to give the scene a super-photographic reality. It was one of the first of the artist's works to enter a museum, being purchased by the city of Pau in 1878.

LIFT FOLD FOR ENTIRE PAINTING —

DETAIL AT RIGHT

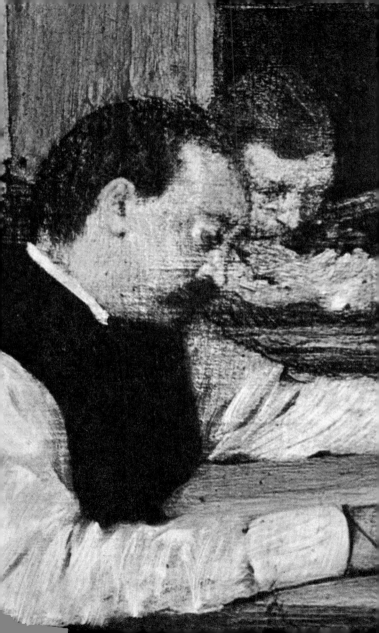

PLATE 21

Painted about 1878–79

REHEARSAL OF BALLET
ON THE STAGE

The Metropolitan Museum of Art, New York
(Havemeyer Collection)

Pastel on paper, 20½ x 27⅞″

Degas found the moment of rehearsal on the stage of
more interest than the finished production of a ballet.
He loved to catch such incongruities as the director in
his black suit among the airy delicacy of the dancers;
he liked to contrast this pair of bored men, looking on
from the wings, with the animation and movement of
the ensemble.

This is more than a simple backstage illustration. The
artist has selected his plunging viewpoint from an opera
box. This allows him to set up a quick, staccato rhythm
of the figures, gathered in a concentric circle round the
director. He has studied the effect of light, contrasting
the radiance of the footlights with the shadowy stage
behind. Over the picture he has shed charming pinks
and greys and delicate greens. Here and there a darker
note is introduced to give character and bring the scene
to life. The masterful strokes of the rhythmic drawing
are even more apparent in pastel than in his oils.

PLATE 22

Painted in 1880

THE DANCING CLASS

Denver Art Museum, Colorado

Pastel on paper, 24¾ x 18⅞″

Degas did more than picture the ballet in its fleeting, ecstatic moments. He observed, with trenchant realism, the hours of preparation in the classroom and the movement of dancers, adjusting their slippers, stretching their muscles, practicing their positions at the bar. He revealed the awkwardness of these performers, finding a new beauty in such truth.

This is a typical snapshot view of a number of seemingly unrelated actions fitted into a design. Degas has pushed his four figures to the right and contrasted the filmy, gauzy costumes of his dancers with the street clothes of the other women. Movement is suggested by the slanting floor and diagonals of wall and bench and by the cutting of the right-hand dancer. The clear, revealing atmosphere bathes the scene in exquisite light, to which the touches of color in the ribbons and hats and costumes contribute their share.

Painted in 1883

BREAKFAST AFTER THE BATH

Collection Mr. and Mrs. Leigh B. Block, Chicago

Pastel on paper, 47⅝ x 36¼"

For over twenty years Degas occupied himself with
original studies of the female nude. Instead of fitting
his women into historical or mythological settings as
the old masters had done, he added a note that was new.
He portrayed, with strength and passion, woman in her
bedroom, in her bath, engaged in all the simple, everyday tasks of combing her hair, toweling herself, twisting, bending, and turning in those energetic actions
which bring out the structure of the body in its play of
muscles and flesh.

This is one of the earliest and most complete state-
ments of the theme. The nude woman, with her moving, agitated outline, is pitted against the calm, column-
like figure of the servant. The naked body is strongly
modeled in broken colors learned from the Impressionists, and certain hues are laid one over another to build
up more solid form and dramatic emphasis.

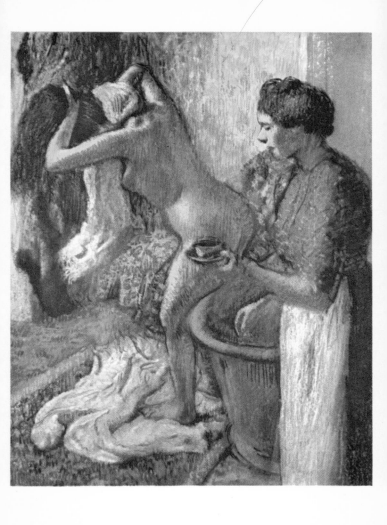

PLATE 24

Painted about 1881–85

JOCKEYS

Yale University Art Gallery, New Haven

Oil on canvas, 10¼ x 15⅜"

As he advanced, Degas concentrated more and more on the fragment. He employed it to suggest a whole composition. Compared with earlier *Jockeys* this daring picture is full of the surprise attack which the artist loved. Only Degas would have thrust the onlooker in among the horses as though he were himself on horseback. Only he would have made the right-hand side of his picture from two enormous heads of horses.

Movement is strongly to the left. The broad, energetic drawing, with its emphasis on outline, is balanced by the use of primary colors in the jackets: red, yellow, and blue. This is a picture of energy; horses and riders moving in a slow procession, close together, almost jostling one another. By this time Degas was replacing the Impressionist technique of color spots and broken light with a heavier, more sculpturesque treatment.

LIFT FOLD FOR ENTIRE PAINTING →

DETAIL AT RIGHT

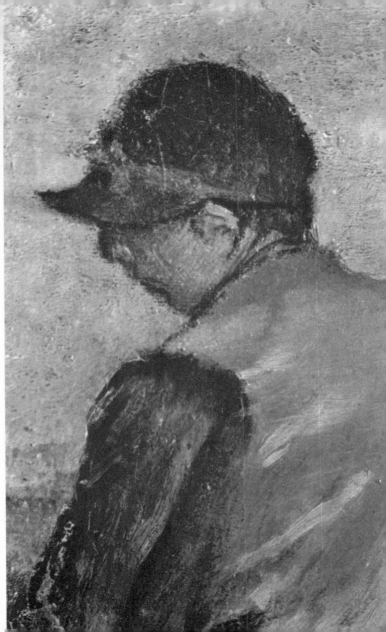

PLATE 25

Painted in 1886

THE TUB

The Louvre, Paris

Pastel on cardboard, 23⅝ x 32⅛"

This is one of the artist's most original variations on his
theme of a woman at her bath. Probably from Japanese
art Degas derived this daring perspective with its tilted
point of view and flattened shelf of toilet articles which
contrast with the curves in the figure and the tin bath-
tub. Always the realist, Degas has made something
solid as well as lovely in surface from the woman's
body. The contour of the bather is most delicately ap-
prehended and the light falls skillfully to model the
full, rounded forms, which, incidentally, echo the
shapes of the pitchers on the shelf. Supple, masterly,
sketchy here, more finished there, is Degas' use of pastel. No artist before or after him discovered such a
range in this difficult medium.

LIFT FOLD FOR ENTIRE PAINTING —
DETAIL AT RIGHT

PLATE 26

Painted about 1884

TWO LAUNDRESSES

The Louvre, Paris

Oil on canvas, 29⅞ x 32¼"

This composition of two laundresses is a rich study of character and counter-movement. Degas has designed the figures in contrast—one stretching and yawning, the other pressing down her iron in vigorous muscular action. Subjects like this had been taboo in painting before the Impressionists, and among his contemporaries Degas was perhaps unique in finding an almost classical form to express so homely a scene from everyday life. Degas here broadened the field of art as Zola broadened the field of the novel.

PLATE 27

Painted in 1885

A BALLET SEEN FROM AN OPERA BOX

John G. Johnson Collection, Philadelphia

Pastel on paper, 25⅛ x 19¼"

Part of Degas' originality lay in finding unusual angles of vision. His snapshot views, his close-ups, his unusual manner of cutting his compositions and tilting them and foreshortening them, all contribute to the surprise effect of such a picture as this. Never before in art had a foreground figure been seen in so fragmentary a form —a partial profile, a fan, and an extended arm with an opera-glass. Our eye travels rapidly over this dark area to focus on the bowing ballet dancer and the whirling figures behind seen in exquisite color and light as only Degas could render them. Such contrived designs suggested the spontaneous movement of life; they were later to be imitated by a whole band of artists starting with Toulouse-Lautrec and are today a commonplace in advertising and photography.

PLATE 28

Painted about 1889

THE MANTE FAMILY

Collection Mrs. Huttleston Rogers, New York

Pastel on paper, 35⅜ x 19⅝"

A delightful picture of a family group in the ballet.
Here Degas has combined elements of portraiture with
types drawn from his backstage experience. The Mantes
were notably connected with the Opera in Paris; the
father played in the orchestra and three of his daughters
were at one time or another dancers in the ballet. The
one in the practice costume is Suzanne, then about
seven; her sister, Blanche, in street clothes, was eight or
nine at the time.

How often must the artist have seen the mothers of
the little ballerinas fastening ribbons in their hair or
tying bows on their shoulders! Here he has contrasted
the child in her dancing costume with the slightly older
sister in street clothes, a contrast subtly felt in the dif-
ference in poses, the one of the left, stolid and waiting,
the *danseuse* already stretching her toe and altogether
more fluid and graceful in the line of her figure.

Painted in 1860

SPARTAN GIRLS AND BOYS EXERCISING

National Gallery, London

Oil on canvas, 42⅞ x 61″

Degas began by trying to be what the French call "a painter of history." This meant choosing a respectable subject, usually from Greek or Roman life, and rendering it in careful modeling based on classical sculpture. Here he has represented Lycurgus and the older women of Sparta watching the girls and boys of the city at their games; at one time he planned to insert the façade of a temple in the center of his design.

But even as a young painter Degas was beginning to study life around him. These adolescents are no longer the petrified figures of the Neo-Classical tradition which had existed in France since the time of David. Degas chose his models from the youngsters of Montmartre and he has accented their Parisian, rather than their Spartan, appearance. Likewise the color is far warmer and more varied than the usual cold tones of academic French art.

Painted about 1860-62

THE BELLELLI FAMILY

The Louvre, Paris

Oil on canvas, 78¾ x 99⅝"

Degas worked off and on for five years painting this ambitious group portrait of his Italian relatives. The design of the picture is based on a series of rectangles, against which play the curves of the figures—a device which the artist imitated from his study of the old masters. More original is Degas' brilliant characterization of the four figures, and the air of subdued drama he manages to inject into this simple domestic scene.

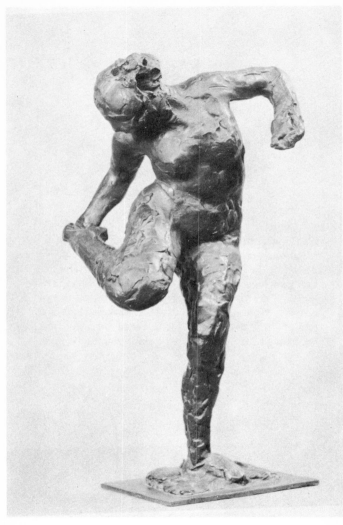

Plate 29. DANCER LOOKING AT HER FOOT. *1900. Bronze*
The Metropolitan Museum of Art, New York

Plate 30. A DANCER AT THE AGE OF FOURTEEN. *1880. Bronze*
The Metropolitan Museum of Art, New York

Degas

Plate 31. DANCER ADJUSTING SLIPPER. *1874. Pencil and chalk*
The Metropolitan Museum of Art, New York

Plate 32. DANCERS. *1879. Charcoal heightened with white*
Wildenstein and Co., New York

Plate 33. STUDY: DIEGO MARTELLI. *About 1879. Pencil*
Fogg Museum, Cambridge, Mass. (Collection Paul J. Sach

Plate 34. SEATED VIOLINIST. *1877–78. Black chalk and pastel*
The Metropolitan Museum of Art, New York

Plate 35. THE LAUNDRESS *(study for plate 26). 1884. Pastel.*

Plate 36. MISS CASSATT AT THE LOUVRE. *1880. Pastel*
Collection Henry P. McIlhenny, Philadelphia, Pa.

Plate 37. STUDIES OF FOUR JOCKEYS. *1886. Oil sketch*
The Art Institute of Chicago (L. L. Coburn Collection)

Plate 38. THREE NUDE DANCERS. *1892–95. Charcoal*
Collection Marcel Bing, Paris

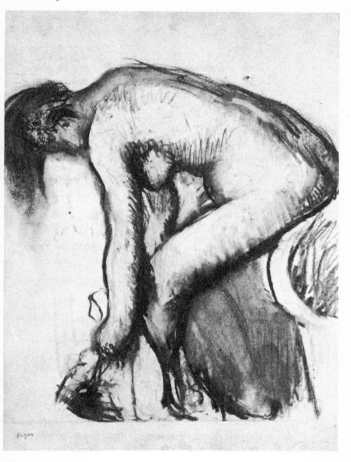

Plate 39. AFTER THE BATH. *About 1895. Charcoal and pastel*
Art Institute of Chicago (Gift of Mrs. Potter Palmer)

ABOUT DEGAS

1834   Degas (pronounced *de-GAH*) born in Paris,
        July 19. Father, a banker, emigrated from
        Italy; mother's family established in New
        Orleans.

1845–53 Enters the Lycée Louis-le-Grand; interested
        in drawing, using family as models, even
        when registered in Faculty of Law in 1853.

1854–58 Travels in Italy; enrolls in École des Beaux-
        Arts; meets Ingres whom he reveres as the
        greatest painter; first acquaintance with Japa-
        nese art, a decisive influence.

1865–71 Exhibits in the Salon; service in artillery dur-
        ing Franco-Prussian War weakens eyesight.

1872–73 Visits New Orleans with brother René.

1874–77 Helps organize and participates in first Impres-
        sionist shows; eyesight continues to fail.

1878–81 Exhibits a statuette; the Museum of Pau buys
        The Cotton Market, New Orleans, first Degas
        to hang in a museum; continues to exhibit with
        Impressionists, now called Independents.

1882–90 Associates but no longer exhibits with Inde-
        pendents; henceforth exhibits only through
        Durand-Ruel. Travels in Spain and Switzer-
        land; leads active social life in Paris; absorbed
        in forming his own collection of paintings.

1892–1909 Paints less and less as eyesight continues to
        fail; oils abandoned for pastels; devotes more
        time to sculpture.

1912	A Degas in the Rouart collection brings about $100,000 at auction.
1914	Isaac de Camondo collection of Degas enters the Louvre.
1917	Dies in Paris, September 27.

DEGAS ON HIS ART

"Art is vice, one does not marry it, one ravishes it."

"No art was ever less spontaneous than mine. What I do is the result of reflection and study of the great masters; of inspiration, spontaneity, temperament I know nothing."

"I am a colorist with line."

"You know what I think of painters who work in the open. If I were the government I would have a company of police watching out for men who paint landscapes from nature. Oh, I don't wish for anybody's death, I should be quite content with a little buckshot to begin with. . . . Renoir, that's different, he can do what he likes."

"A picture is first of all a product of the imagination of the artist; it must never be a copy. If then two or three natural accents can be added, obviously no harm is done. The air we see in the paintings of the old masters is never the air we breathe."

"It is much better to draw only what remains in the memory. It is a transformation during which imagination collaborates with memory; you reproduce only what strikes the eye, that is to say, the necessary. Thus, one's recollections and invention are freed from nature's tyranny."

OTHER BOOKS ABOUT DEGAS

Edgar Degas. *Letters,* edited by Marcel Guérin. New York, Studio Publications, 1948

P. A. Lemoisne. *Degas et son oeuvre.* Paris, Paul Brame et C. M. de Hauke, 1947–49
(Standard catalogue of Degas' work)

J. B. Manson. *The Life and Work of Edgar Degas.* London, The Studio Limited, 1927

John Rewald. *The History of Impressionism.* New York, The Museum of Modern Art, 1946
(Authoritative history of the movement)

Daniel Catton Rich. *Degas* (The Library of Great Painters). New York, Harry N. Abrams, 1951

ACKNOWLEDGMENTS

In a book of art, it seems particularly fitting to acknowledge the work of craftsmen who contribute to its making. The color plates were made by Litho-Art, Inc., New York. The lithography is from the presses of The Meehan-Tooker Co., Inc., New York and the binding has been done by F. M. Charlton Co., New York. The paper was made by P. H. Glatfelter Co., Spring Grove, Pa. Our deepest indebtedness is to the museums, galleries, and private collectors who graciously permitted the reproduction of their paintings, drawings, and sculpture.